100 Ways

TO BE

That Girl

FIONA FERRIS

Contents

100 Ways to be That Girl *7*

50 Ways to be your own Main Character *73*

To Finish *89*

About the Author *93*

Other books by Fiona Ferris *95*

FIONA FERRIS

Dear lovely reader,

Who or what is *that girl*? You may have heard of her as an online trend. And, if you're a little older like I am, perhaps you watched a television program of the same name in the late 1960s starring Marlo Thomas. She was the original *that girl*!

That girl is the name for someone who has it all going on. She is focused on self-improvement, is supremely organized, and well put-together too. She works out regularly and has tons of energy. She does all those wellness things that we mean to get around to doing but never do... such as yoga and stretching daily. And she does all of this without showing off; it's just what she does. Maybe we know people like this in our real life and wonder how they do it all!

So I thought it would be a fun idea for a mini-book to focus on getting some 'that girl' energy for ourselves. Sure we may love our lazy life; I certainly like to keep my life as simple, low-key, and yes, as relaxed as possible, but at the same time it's fun to zing things up a little. We can enjoy our comfortable down-time *and* be *that girl*. We want it all and there is absolutely no reason why we shouldn't have it!

Our inner *that girl* is *great* at motivating us when we really want to gain some traction but inertia is holding us back. She is our alter ego, our greatest cheerleader and she makes it fun to take action. She gives us great ideas and helps us carry them through. She wakes us up early and gets us to make our bed before we've even had a shower. Just who is this girl? She's *that girl*!

And we don't have to look at the perfect online influencers and celebrities to inspire us either. Too often they are the opposite of inspiring, especially if we're in a lower state of mind. We think, 'I'll never be like that, I may as well finish off this block of chocolate'. Nope, we can be 'her' ourselves, *in our own way*, and still eat chocolate too (yay!) We can become the embodiment of our own *that girl* and live the life of our dreams, whatever that looks like for us.

How I live my life and also what I put into my books (because they're the same thing), is that I like any self-improvement projects to be fun, enjoyable, easy *and* not cost a bomb. I love goal setting and creating my dream life, and I also like to fit my desires in with my energy levels, money available, and time too.

It doesn't matter your age, your size, or your cultural background. You can be the *that girl* of your own life, the leading lady in your own movie. There is no one size fits all, so I thought it would be a fun project to marry *that girl* inspiration with real life practicality for the ultimate in easy, fun, and aspirational results.

So get your gear on, we're heading into *that girl* territory. It's going to be a super-cool ride. Now let's immerse ourselves in one-hundred ways to be * ***that girl*** *. Such fun! I'm so glad you're here with me.

Fiona

100 Ways to be That Girl

1.   **Define *that girl* for yourself**. What is your idea of what it means to be *that girl*? You will find it illuminating if you ask yourself this question and write down what comes to you. When I did it, I got that she listens to herself more than she listens to others' opinions. She decides for herself who she wants to be and what she wants her ideal lifestyle to look like, even if it might seem silly to others. She does what makes her happy. She loves to be healthier and looks for ways to improve on her fitness and health all the time. She has fun with whatever she does. She is savvy with money and funds her lifestyle wisely. And she pampers herself with self-care regularly – daily if possible. Spend five minutes thinking

about this for yourself and see the wisdom and simplicity that will show itself to you.

2. **Make healthy habits your top priority**. Good health ultimately contributes to desirable *that girl* attributes such as vibrancy, vivaciousness, and high energy. So begin your *that girl* journey by considering how you can infuse your daily routine with healthy lifestyle choices. Make a list of areas you desire to improve in and start from there. Don't try to completely revolutionize how you live, simply choose one tiny habit change and start with that. After three weeks of consistency with that habit, choose another to add in. Simple upgrades to start with might be changing out soda for sparkling water, or going for a ten minute walk outside every day no matter the weather. The smaller the habit the better; everything adds up.

3. **Be the most organized person you know**. *That girl* has her life sorted. She knows where her bills are at, and most of the time her laundry is up-to-date. Her house always has a reasonable level of tidiness. She loves the feeling of having her life in order and being on top of daily admin. She knows she just feels happier and more content being organized than not. Commit to sorting out all your loose ends and incompletes. Make yourself a big list

and start working your way through it. Either tick them off, delegate them to someone else, or even just delete them if something has timed itself out. As well, simplify things as you go, so there is less to take care of in the future.

4.   **Embrace an air of positivity**. No matter how negative people are around you, no matter how much they complain about their lives, you don't need to join in. You are a divine creature who hovers above this earth in your bubble of optimism! You are kind towards others, but you do not let yourself be distracted or brought down by engaging in complaining, negative talk or looking at the bad side of a situation. There is nothing to be gained, plus it feels horrible. Instead, raise your attitude to rival Pollyanna; be grateful for your wonderful life even if it feels pretty ordinary. Life is good! And a habit of positivity will make it even better.

5.   **Start each day off well**. Work out how best you like to start your day and see if you can make it happen *often*. I like to get up early but get going slowly. I start with a big cup of hot tea and I either read, write or journal. I work from home now, but even when I had to be in the office at 8am I got up extra early just so I could read a book leisurely with my breakfast at the kitchen table. Come up with all the

things which would make a great start to your day and try to do them as much as possible.

6. **Be your own influencer**. Rather than buy what those people on Instagram are sponsored to sell you, why not curate your own must-haves? Streamline down to your absolute favourites and use those. Sell them to yourself when you are tempted to spend your money on something promoted by others. When you do see an interesting product, take note but don't jump in straight away. Others are drawn to us when we are unique and discerning rather than being just like everyone else. There is nothing so alluring than someone with their own point of view who runs on a different track to everyone else. Be that girl yourself.

7. **Move habitually**. I get so bored doing formal exercise and it seems such a waste of my time, although I do go for a walk most days, and sometimes I'll even remember to pick up my mini hand weights and do a few arm lifts. But when you think about it, movement keeps your body limber, your blood circulating, and oxygen flowing. So, why not dance around waiting for the kettle to boil for a cup of tea? Do a little boogie on the way to the kitchen when the ads are on television? Stand up and give yourself a huge luxurious stretch while a photo is uploading to your social? (I live in the

country and the Internet is slow, you may be luckier!) Do some ballet poses even though you have never studied ballet in your life (I haven't, it doesn't stop me). *That girl* is always on the move. She stays flexible. She is free-flowing and easy in her body.

8. **Adopt your own *that girl* aesthetic**. Why not have a little fun designing your life? When you need something new, choose the option that rings your bell from the selection available, whether it's a candle, journal, or pair of workout leggings. Don't be afraid to mix new ideas into your current style, thus moving with the times and living in the present moment rather than 'how you've always been'. It's all very well to love your personal style and desire to be 'a classic dresser' always, but maybe there are details you can upgrade from time to time to stay *au courant*. There's just something fun about being aware of what is going on. I am a slow adopter of trends mostly, but sometimes I'll catch onto something straight away and it feels good. If you're feeling a little bored with your look, whether it's your home or in your closet, ask your inner *that girl* for a boost, and take note when she points out little updates you could make.

9. **Let people be who they are**. I had a recent situation where someone I thought was a

friend became more and more distant, for whatever reason. For a long time I stewed about it, wondering what I'd done wrong and wanting to ask them. But also not wanting to ask because I knew I'd come across desperate and needy! How I eventually got over myself, because I already knew it was a lot more to do with what was going on in her own life rather than anything I'd done or not done, was to recategorize her. Rather than considering her a friend, I now see her as an acquaintance. An acquaintance to me is the type you are happy to see and have a chat with when you end up at the same event, but outside of that you don't see each other. As opposed to a friend who you text with regularly, and meet up for coffee etc. When I did this, nothing changed for the other person, because she was just living her life. But for me, it made me feel a million times better. I would highly recommend doing this if you find yourself continually hurt by someone who is less invested in the relationship than you are, regardless if it's a family member or friend. Because *that girl* never chases a relationship.

10. **Be financially savvy**. *That girl* is not broke because she spent all her money on a designer handbag and doesn't have enough left over for groceries. She likes nice things of course, but she also loves to get the most she can from

every dollar and makes wise money decisions. She saves up for the things she wants, and loves to plan for a wealthier future by inspiring herself with financial books that resonate with her. There is no need for money to be intimidating or dry and dusty. Money can be a fun key to your most fabulous life. (I wrote a book all about this called *Financially Chic*. Look it up if you need some inspiration in this area.) Decide for yourself that you are going to become someone who is savvier in your personal finances. Look up YouTube videos, read books, and follow people on social media who are heading in the direction that you'd like to be going in too.

11. **Become a living embodiment of your vision board**. Take a look at your boards on Pinterest, or perhaps your collection of torn-out magazine pages. See the recipes and outfit inspiration photos you've saved. Do they resemble your wardrobe or how you eat? Try to bring your real life and your idealistic life closer together and consider that *how you live* could be your vision board: how you decorate your home, how you dress, and how you dine. Be inspired to become a walking, talking, living embodiment of your dream life, the one you write about in your journal. Doesn't this sound more fun than a strict diet and punishing to-do lists?

12. **Design your own morning routine**. *That girl* has a morning routine that she devised for herself and *she adores it*. She was inspired by all the books and social channels which talk about the perfect morning routine, then she threw that all out the window and designed a morning that was perfect for *her*. When I worked at a nine-to-five job, my morning routine started early, with a cup of tea and writing before work. Then I had a shower, and ate breakfast while reading a book. I would take my book on the bus too, and by the time I arrived at work I felt like I'd had a leisurely morning and was ready to start my day. Now I work from home, but my day starts off the same. I rise at 6am and go straight to my office with a large mug of tea. I write for a couple of hours, then take a walk on our treadmill while I watch a television program or movie. Then it's smoothie time, shower time and get on with the rest of my day time. Ponder what elements would set you up for a good day and see if you can incorporate them into your morning. Five minutes of stretching sounds like a nice addition to mine!

13. **Consider aesthetics in everything you do**. *That girl* likes things to look nice. She values beauty and takes the time to put together pleasing looks whether it's on her dinner plate, styling her bed when she makes

it, or when choosing an outfit. She keeps her bathroom vanity clear and displays just a few pretty items. She cleans and tidies daily and prefers a luxe, minimal style. Look around your environment and see if there are any little touches you can add – or subtract – to elevate your décor. Modernise your aesthetic too – are there youthful, on-trend touches that you can update your look with in small and inexpensive ways?

14. **Take time for yourself**. *That girl* knows that in order to be in her best energy for others, she needs to prioritize herself. She takes bubble baths, applies face masks, and disappears for a few hours of window shopping every so often. She spends time organizing her closet for the new season, enjoys applying her makeup in the morning and makes simple and delicious meals even if it's just her there. *She does not judge certain activities as frivolous.* Doing nice things for herself is a regular occurrence, not a twice-yearly thing. They don't have to be big or time-consuming, nor even cost money. But the fact that she is mindful of her own needs means she is a happier person. There is no martyrish resentment necessary when you're *that girl*!

15. **Wear a scrunchie**. If your hair is long enough for a ponytail, go and take a look at all

the beautiful scrunchies that are available these days. Or, if you're a sewer, you can make your own. I know you're not supposed to wear a trend you wore the first time around but I've decided to ignore that 'rule' and now have many cute scrunchies. Most I only wear at home, but I do have a few that I wear in public. And I've just bought a beautiful deep brown velvet scrunchie which has several gold rings around it. I think it will be perfect for autumn dressing. And one big bonus is that a scrunchie is kinder on your hair than elastics.

16. **Up your water game**. We all know that water is great for the trillions of cells in our body, and it will make us smarter, prettier, and healthier. But sometimes we can just... forget to drink it. Firstly, work out how much you want to drink. For me, I feel best when I sip between two and three litres per day (67-100 fluid ounces). Then, choose how and when you're going to drink it: in a water bottle on your desk, hot lemon water in the morning, sparkling water instead of alcohol, and herbal tea after dinner. There are so many ways in which you can make sure you get the amount of water you need, without feeling like you're constantly sipping all day. And if you don't 'want' to drink water, it just doesn't appeal to you; remember, you're *that girl*. She does what is important. She is hydrated. She glows!

17. **Be your own dream girl**. When you are your own dream girl, you know what's right for you. Others may give you well-meaning (unsolicited) advice and you politely say thank you, but then you do exactly as you please. To become your own dream girl requires you to love yourself, big-time, to fill yourself with pleasure, to own your flavour of beauty, and to let go of what others may expect of you. Most importantly, being your own dream girl means you need to show up for yourself in the key areas of your life. You must stop letting yourself down! I know it's hard to hear, don't worry, I'm talking to myself too. In order to disregard what others might say, we need to *regard* what we desire for ourselves.

18. **Make shower time pampering time**. Maybe you're a bath girl where you get your soaking time, but I've always loved showers. So how I get my pampering in is to stock my shower with lovely goodies. Yes, I may take longer than the average person in the shower, but it's worth it to me. In my shower I have two types of shampoos (one is a purple shampoo), conditioner, facial wash, facial scrub/clay mask, shower gel, soap, a pumice stone, claw clip, and a poufy netting body brush. All of these things are used every week. I wash and condition my hair every two or three days, and I clip my hair up while it conditions. I alternate

my face products, and use my body brush every day. The pumice is used on my heels once or twice a week, more in the summer. Having my showering pamper time sets me up for a great day, and helps me feel more like *that girl*. It's my own little spa retreat each morning.

19. **Find an hour in every day**. Sometimes the day goes by so quickly, and in a heartbeat it's time for dinner and bed. Instead of letting the day rule you, take an investigative approach and see where time is slipping through your fingers. And then, choose an hour just for you. You might want to start a writing routine, so tell yourself that at 7pm each night you will write for an hour. Or you might desire more time to read, journal and *just be,* so do that. Maybe you want an hour to have a bath, work on your to-do list for tomorrow, or do some meal prepping. Whatever would make you feel like you're living your best *that girl* life, do *that* in your reclaimed hour!

20. **Always be growing**. *That girl* is a life-long learner. She knows her education didn't finish at school; she was *just getting started*. I never particularly enjoyed high school; it was just so boring, even though I like being able to spell and do maths. I did well in most of my classes, but I felt like real life was waiting out there for

me to join in. And I didn't go to University either. But I have always been interested in bettering myself. Since I was a little girl I have been a keen reader of both fiction and non-fiction. I studied self-development from my early twenties, when course material came on cassette tapes in the mail! And I was always in the public library on my lunch break. These days I still read a lot, purchase online courses I am interested in, and listen to self-development talks on YouTube. Find topics or skills *you* are interested in learning about and study them. Embody what you learn and apply it to your life too.

21. **Wear what makes you feel good**. We all know how a fab outfit can make us feel – like we can handle anything. Can we all vow to ourselves that we are going to wear those clothes more often and not save them for 'best'? Every day is our best day! *That girl* would never get around in sub-par clothes while her gorgeous threads are hanging up gathering dust. I know for those of us who are thrifty, we don't want to wear our good clothes out or 'waste' them. But life isn't never-ending. And neither are trends, no matter how classic our taste is. Plus our body shape may change over time too. So find out what makes you feel amazing, and wear those outfits today, and every day. Make it your *goal* to wear them out!

22. **Put your dreams and goals first**. It doesn't matter what others want. You don't need to have the same desires as they do. Others might not get you. They might think that what you dream of isn't possible or that it's silly. But that's only because they want something different. When my husband Paul and I lived in the city, the general vibe there was going bigger, getting ahead and living that fast-paced city life. We decided that we wanted something different, and moved to the small provincial area where I grew up so we could live our life in a slower manner. I was just lucky that Paul wanted the same thing, because even when I lived in the city as a single girl I desired a small-town life. It was always my goal. Whatever *you* want, work on making it your reality, because not only is it possible, it's what you *require*.

23. **'Book in' all your little pampering appointments**. Whether they are at home or in a salon, make a 'schedule' and stick to it. I like to paint my nails once a week, do a face mask in the shower once or twice a week, and spend time blow-drying my hair after I wash it every three days. I tint my own eyebrows once a month and epilate my legs monthly too (with the occasional shave to exfoliate and avoid ingrown hairs). I also love putting my makeup on in the morning, even if I'm not going

anywhere. All the little things that make you feel wonderful, keep them up. They aren't just for vanity, they will also help you deal with stress, feel more positive, and improve your body image. Pampering enriches your life so much; make sure you keep yours up!

24. **Be your own best friend**. *That girl* doesn't put herself down or make self-deprecating remarks. But neither is she stuck up or over-confident. She simply endeavours to be a best friend to herself: a cheerleader, coach, and someone who can be counted on to provide a needed pep talk. She knows she is only human, so while she expects a lot from herself, she is also forgiving. What this looks like in my life is that I make time to rest and play, as well as do my work. I'm kind to myself most of the time. I know I can't be expected to be perfect and sometimes I'll just say something really dumb. I did this yesterday and stewed on it all day, but today I've let it go. A best friend would do that for me!

25. **Make a healthy diet enjoyable**. *That girl* knows that eating healthy will give her the energy and happiness to live her best life, but she doesn't just want to go around eating plain salads and boring protein. So she looks on Pinterest for ideas and zings up her meals both by how they look (sprinkling with edible

flowers and finely chopped bright green herbs), and how they taste (adding delicious seasonings). She has her favourite standby meals, and she also researches new recipes. The key for her is to find foods that excite her tastebuds but that are also beneficial to her body. Be *that girl* when you are shopping for groceries. Have high standards. Choose to be healthy. Spend on fresh treats such as raspberries in season rather than on junk food. Junk in, junk out. Goodness in, goodness out!

26. **Have fun every day**. In our ideal lifestyle, we will have the self-improvement goals we desire to align with, such as being more organized, moving our body, and meal-prepping etc, but we also want to *have fun*. For some of us, we are so involved with getting through our day, we've forgotten what fun looks like, and worse, can feel guilty if we do something purely for enjoyment. Like we're slacking off or something! But life shouldn't be a burden, we do get to play and receive pleasure as well. So dream up all the activities you find enjoyable, and do something every day that brings your idealistic way of life into reality.

27. **Choose your own way**. *That girl* doesn't rush out and buy a diet book and follow their plan. She doesn't follow a six-step blueprint leading her to her dream life. She doesn't build

her wardrobe based on 'ten pieces every woman should own'. Instead she marches to the beat of her own drum. She asks *herself* what would suit her best. She calls on her future self for advice. She asks herself what would be helpful in a certain situation. And then she listens. You will be amazed that you have all the answers too. You can't not. They have been encoded into you from birth, and you only need to ask. You get to have it any way you want. You get to choose. You can't do it wrong!

28. **Take a Hot Girl Walk**. I came across this wellness trend and thought it was so cute! And such an amusing tongue-in-cheek name too. A Hot Girl Walk is when you walk for about an hour, and listen to something inspirational. The 'rules' are that you can only think about three things on your walk: 1) what you are grateful for, 2) your goals and how you would love to achieve them, and 3) how hot you are. Isn't that fun? Of course, the target demographic for this trend is way younger than I am, but then I thought, Why *not* me? Are positivity and playful activities limited only to the youth? Imagine walking for an hour pumping your confidence up with positive affirmations. And if you did it daily? I reckon you'd become unstoppable.

29. **Make your bed as soon as you rise**. There is something about a neatly made bed that lifts the spirits. You can't help but feel calmed as you glimpse it through the day. I used to fold my top layer back and wait for our bed to 'air' but really, how much airing does a bed need? I think it was just a procrastination tactic. These days I make my bed as early in the day as I can. I'm not perfect about it and some days I leave it hanging around for a while. But mostly it's made early, and looks lovely for me to enjoy for longer. It's not just about the bed either. Making your bed early each day sets you up for success – it's a motivating habit which increases your self-esteem. And you receive visual calm which soothes your nervous system. I even read that people who make their beds each day become better with money. I don't know exactly how that would be, but why not try it? I know many of you will already make your bed each day, like I do. But for me, keeping these points in mind will encourage me to make it sooner. Not *after my shower*, or *after breakfast*. What I do know is that *that girl's* bed is always neatly and beautifully made, with the simple addition of a decorative pillow or two. Of course it is!

30. **Learn about yourself**. *That girl* knows that to live a wonderful life, she needs to focus on being her best self and is a keen proponent of

self-improvement. She knows that inner work is the key to living well, looking glowy, and being her happiest self. What kind of self-development we prefer will differ for each of us, but the types I love best are journalling inspiration, listening to YouTube videos of positive people (Dawn from *The Minimal Mom* is great), and reading or listening to audiobooks (authors such as Rhonda Byrne, Brian Tracy, Darren Hardy, Denise Duffield-Thomas, and Napoleon Hill). I also enjoy self-study, working through courses I've bought, or studying books such as *Style Statement* by Carrie McCarthy and Danielle LaPorte, and Alexandra Stoddard's *Daring To Be Yourself*. *French Lessons* by EJ Gore is a lovely book with many journal prompts in it too. It's such a fun indulgence to retreat into your own inner world and work out exactly what *you* love and how *you* want to live.

31. **Choose a wellness bowl for lunch**. Instead of making a salad because 'it's healthy', or eating something less nutritious because you 'feel like it', create your own wellness bowl. There are tons of ideas online, and you can devise your own from ingredients you prefer. Shifting my thought from, 'What should I have for lunch?' to 'What should I put in my wellness bowl?' helps me come up with different ideas such as creating an

aesthetically pleasing bowl, and adding extra touches like a sprinkling of toasted sesame seeds. You can prepare components ahead of time such as toasting the seeds, roasting pumpkin cubes in balsamic vinegar, washing and spinning your lettuce pieces or other leafy greens, and cooking your protein to go with it. That way you only have to compile your wellness bowl at lunchtime. *That girl* loves a good wellness bowl, and they are so good for her too!

32. **Consider yourself a mentor**. You might not think many people notice you, but they do. Whether you are at home, work, or out at the shops, people can see you. Many will look up to you, which is a responsibility to be taken seriously! Act as if you are that quietly influential person, a lady of self-possession. Dress the part, speak the part, and remember your power. There is no need to instruct anyone or tell them what to do; you can inspire them simply by the way you are being. The bonus is that when you live your life as if you were a mentor to others, you will increase your own happiness too.

33. **Make betterment your hobby**. Instead of having a to-do list or habit tracker where your self-improvement efforts become just another thing you need to tick off before the end of the

day, incorporate your desired goals into your normal routine. That way, you do things automatically and enjoyably, and they become a hobby not a chore. What this looks like for me is that I start each day lighting a scented candle or filling up my essential oil diffuser, putting on soft background music, and switching on lamps. I also play audiobooks or podcasts while I do household tasks such as laundry or cleaning up the kitchen. I wear my nicer clothes and put on makeup even for a day at home. I declutter and tidy most days to keep my home looking nice. And I consider my writing time *relaxing time*. It's my 'work' but I also can't wait to get back to it. Find the spots in your day that feel like a bit of a slog and breathe new life into them.

34. **Cultivate a soft life**. 'Soft life' is another current trendy phrase that I just adore. I've never looked up the exact meaning of it because it seems self-explanatory to me. It speaks of living in a softer way, being gentle with yourself, surrounding yourself with comfort and textures that bring about a feeling of cozy, and of living in the moment. I can almost imagine a misty-filtered lens on my day when I'm living a soft life! In writing this book I *did* look up the definition, and the dictionary says 'a soft life refers to a lifestyle of comfort and relaxation with minimal challenges or

stress. Some people use the term in reference to a life that involves (and is a product of) wealth and luxury, while others interpret it as a simplified life unburdened from stress and responsibilities.' I can see how both would be applicable, but for me, a simplified life sounds wonderful. Which definition would you choose for yourself?

35. **Express gratitude**. There is something about saying 'thank you' to the Universe, God, or whoever you choose. I used to think that gratitude was... a little trite, but there really is a shift that happens when you do it. Something changes inside of you and you become happier. The lens you see your life through becomes cleaner and brighter – colours really do pop! And more goodness seems to come to you too. That's why I enjoy listening to Rhonda Byrne's audiobooks when I'm feeling blah – her constant message of gratefulness lifts me up again and I see the world from where I know I am meant to see it – from the penthouse level instead of a damp basement. And you can do this for yourself too, by saying 'thank you' every day. I say it in my mind, out loud, to myself, and to others. *Thank you for this day. Thank you for my life. Thank you for my delicious breakfast. Thank you for my safe home. Thank you for my pets. Thank you for my fridge full of food. Thank you for my*

lovely clothes. Thank you for the money in my bank account. No matter how much or how little we have, we can be thankful.

36. **Read books**. *That girl* is a voracious reader. You can imagine her curled up at home or taking sun at a park, paper book in hand. She increases her world through her mind. She reads up on topics which interest her. She loses herself in a novel. And maybe she'll read on her Kindle too. She knows that scrolling and excess screen time feels draining to her. It feels like she is taking in empty calories no matter how inspiring the content may be. There is just something about a book to her that is slower, whether it's on a paper page or an eReader screen. It's not the latest breaking news. A book could have been written one month ago or one hundred years ago. The words are permanent and stable. They are not edited or updated to reflect recent trends or events. She knows she can rely on a book to be a snapshot in time and there is something very calming about that. Sometimes books feel too 'slow', and this is how she knows that it is *exactly* the time she needs to read a book instead of going to her iPad.

37. **Be the main character in your life**. Just like in a movie, *you* are the main character of your life. (Everyone gets to be!) Rather than

worry about how others perceive you or what they might think about your choices, focus on what *you* need, and how you desire to live. Establish boundaries to protect yourself; actually ponder in your journal what those boundaries might look like. When you do things like this you will radiate 'main character energy'. Not only will you feel happier overall, because you are the one in charge of your destiny, but those around you will see you differently too because you are showing up differently. They may appear to have more respect and reverence for you. It's not something you need to do strongly and obviously, just a dash is enough for lasting effect.

38. **Create your own balance**. *That girl* has great self-confidence, but she ensures that she never tips over into show-off territory. The word *insouciant* was made for her. She just has those cool vibes which makes people wonder how she got to be how she is. She is friendly without being clingy, and you know she is genuinely interested when she speaks with you. She leaves a lasting impression on whoever she is with through her presence, grace, and charisma. Find your own balance of being kind without being a pushover, confident without being overbearing, and

focused on your goals while still maintaining a sense of play and fun.

39. **Be unique**. An important attribute of *that girl* is that she doesn't mind being *different* to other people. She has her own point of view, and is passionate about what she believes in. While still listening to others, she has her own interests, hobbies, and standards. And she owns *all* parts of herself. For me, I talk too much sometimes, I get loud and excitable, I'm curvy not pin-thin, and my hair has a mind of its own. But they are all part of *me* so why would I disown them? When you think about it like that, owning your uniqueness is the ultimate act of self-love. And when you love yourself, it means others can too. Be uniquely, beautifully you. Shine your light!

40. **Don't be a victim**. Blaming other people or circumstances for all that is wrong in your life is not a *that girl* vibe. What is, is focusing on the positive in people, taking responsibility for all you have achieved as well as your failings (consider them a learning experience), and looking on the bright side of life, always. The first step is to recognize when you're doing it, because for some of us it can be a habitual way of thinking. This awareness alone will help a lot. And when you do, you can redirect yourself. Consider the opposite of the word

'victim' – why not choose to be a *victor* or a *winner* instead? Have a mantra you repeat, such as 'I am in control of my own destiny', 'No-one gets to make me feel bad', or 'I prefer to feel good!' When I'm feeling down about something I like to say, 'It's only temporary'.

41. **Be *that girl* at any age**. I am well aware that at fifty-two I am probably more than double the age of *that girl*. But does this minor point stop me from being inspired to take a Hot Girl Walk, curate my own *that girl* aesthetic and make a green smoothie? *Not at all*. I love to feel youthful in my own way, tapping into the younger trends and adapting them to suit how I like to live, and looking to fast fashion for cues as to what's hot. I can still dress in the boho-classic style I love, but I get to incorporate little details to keep my look feeling fresh. Why should girls in their twenties have all the fun! No matter your age, you can be *that girl*. You can choose to borrow from her mindset, her way of dressing, or how she keeps her home. I live in a normal house in a small town in New Zealand, but in my mind I might reside in a chic Brooklyn, NY apartment, just for the day. Because, why not?

42. **Prioritize your health**. With any decision you make, consider it from a health perspective. With this one 'simple' change, you

can improve your health almost effortlessly. It's not necessarily an easy thing to do, but it is worth practising. And the more you do it, the easier it gets. Imagine lunch out with friends, you'd choose the healthier option on the menu. Or deciding to go for a walk versus scrolling your phone on the sofa. Or deciding whether to accept an invitation to a dinner where you know there will be stressful drama. *I'm so sorry, I can't make it*! Just keep in mind, 'My health is my number one priority', and go from there. You can't go wrong.

43. **Have patience**. *That girl* is always on the improve and loves to find ways to make her life better. But don't make it a race! And don't try to change everything all at once. Far better to choose one thing, such as eating healthier, exercising daily for twenty minutes, or drinking two large bottles of water each day. Take your time and let new upgrades be gentle and fun. Whenever you get that overwhelmed 'I should be doing more' feeling, come back to your one current self-improvement goal. 'Ah that's right, I'm drinking more water today, let's go and get ourselves a glass'.

44. **Become a smoothie girl**. I know they are so trendy, but after I was given a NutriBullet for Christmas several years back, my life has never been the same. Even my husband loves

smoothies for their taste and nutritional benefits. Our everyday morning smoothie contains spinach, seasonal fruit, protein powder, raw nuts and seeds, and a dash of olive oil. A smoothie is delicious, fills you up until your next meal, and is nutrient-rich from all the different ingredients. I honestly feel the difference in zingy energy levels when I have a smoothie versus when I don't. So make like *that girl* and get your green smoothie on!

45. **Learn to love yourself**. *That girl* knows life becomes easier when you choose to be your own best friend. You have your own back! You know you're not perfect, but instead of always criticising yourself and saying, 'You should be better,' you are kind and gentle with yourself, and encouraging too. You want the best for your friend, and you won't hear a bad word said about her. You support her when she wants to try something new, and you say nice things to her when she's down. When she's falling asleep at night you whisper in her ear all the wins she's had that day and how much goodness she has in her life. Imagine having a friend as loving as that. Oh wait, we can, to ourselves!

46. **Create a beautiful evening routine**. Don't you think morning routines get all the glory? They're everywhere! So how about devising

your own peaceful, restorative *evening routine*
to set you up for success? Not only will you
improve your sleep, but you will get a head
start on the next day in terms of knowing what
you're doing, having your outfit ready, and
maybe even a list of your three most important
tasks. I don't choose my clothes for the next
day, but I do keep my closet tidy, with my
everyday clothes front and centre. And they're
all mix-and-match so it's nice and easy. I do
enjoy my leisurely face cleaning time in the
bathroom though, that is a non-negotiable for
me. It takes me at least twenty minutes by the
time I have flossed and brushed my teeth (I
floss first!) and cleansed and moisturised my
face. I also apply a lusciously creamy
moisturizer to my decolletage, hands and feet.
In my ideal evening routine there is 'spa time'
every night and I love it. What does your
evening routine include?

47. **Surround yourself with cozy textures**.
    As humans we are naturally drawn to softness.
    When we pat a cat, we exclaim, 'Her fur is so
    soft!' Create as many areas as possible in your
    life that feel soft too. Whenever you need to
    buy something, choose which feels the most
    delicious. Pamper yourself any way you can.
    Sleep in the softest nightwear, slip your feet
    into furry slides, and wrap up in a white
    towelling robe after your bath. Relax at home

in soft knit loungewear and cozy up in a faux fur throw rug. Declutter any fabrics that don't feel good – clothes, pillows and sheets that feel scratchy – because life is too short to have anything irritate you, no matter how small. Remember the saying, 'It isn't the mountain ahead that wears you out—it's the grain of sand in your shoe.' Remove all the grains of sand from your life starting with what touches your skin.

48. **Create your own healthy lifestyle**. *That girl* has a healthy lifestyle for sure, but we don't need to copy hers exactly to be successful. We can design our own, just for us. Doesn't that sound fun? And very bespoke and luxurious? Imagine being so uber-rich that you would simply say what you want and others will make it happen. Well, I think the 'saying what you want' is the most important part, and the 'happening' will happen when you've decided. So take some time in your journal to brainstorm, 'What does my ideal healthy lifestyle look like?' You will then have your own personalized blueprint to follow. Mine would include going for a walk each day, drinking enough water, making good sleep a priority, having my five-plus fruits and vegetables, and enjoying free time to read or sew. What about you?

49. **Use what you already have**, and be grateful that you have it. Becoming your own *that girl* doesn't mean rushing out to buy new items in the desired aesthetic. For me, it means streamlining and organizing my home, using all the lovely things I own, and appreciating them too. That way, when I do need something new, I can enjoy the shopping and choosing without feeling guilty over unnecessary spending. Plus, my home is nicely uncluttered and has a peaceful, clean feeling about it because I haven't been filling it up unintentionally. There are endless areas in which to enjoy what you already have, such as cosmetics and toiletries, food and drink, clothing, décor, books, and craft supplies.

50. **Find your most productive time of day**. I love getting up early and going to bed at a reasonable time, and my favourite time to be productive is in the morning. If you are a night person you might come alive after dinner. Identify your most productive time and make the most of it, even if other people don't understand. I write from 6am to 9am most days, and sometimes throughout the day too, but another writer I know loves to write after 9pm when her children have gone to bed, and her husband is watching television. We're all different, but what I do know is that 3pm seems to be a major slump time for most!

Identify when you're at your best and do your most important work then.

51. **Have an inspiring list of tv shows**. I love to spark myself up with television shows or movies where the main characters are sassy and unbothered. One of my favourites is Blair Waldorf in the original *Gossip Girl* series. Whatever your preferred feel-good viewings are, revisit them often. I always find my confidence is boosted when I am 'around' these people. It's a funny thing to say, but it's true! And sometimes I don't even need to watch the program, I can just channel a favourite character for a little added oomph. Who we surround ourselves with influences us, so it's important for me to be around kick-ass, can-do, positive, funny ladies!

52. **Wear a pair of white casual shoes**. To update your look (no matter the outfit) find your ideal pair of white lace-up shoes. Keep the style simple and have minimal colour on them. I have a pair of platform-sole white Pumas with the tiniest dash of pink which feel youthful, fresh, and modern to me. I wear them with jeans, but have seen other ladies pair them with skirts or dresses. My mother embraced the white athletic shoe trend far before me and always looks comfortable and stylish when she wears hers. They update any

look in an instant! The bonus is that this style of shoe is *so comfortable*. Maybe you already have a pair of white lace-up casual shoes that you can incorporate into your look in a different way.

53. **Fall madly in love with yourself**. Imagine if you treated yourself like someone you've just met and have a wild crush on. You'd think about them all the time, doodle your name and theirs together, wonder what they're doing right now, and drop everything when they call. Or perhaps you'd play it cooler, being busy and happy when they pop around, always on point with your looks, and playing the long game by not seeing them too often. However you would act in your daydreams, do it for yourself. For me, I'd look good every day, take myself out on solo dates, do things that I know I love doing, and make myself my favourite meals. It's such a fun concept to treat yourself as the one you're trying to impress, don't you think?

54. **Upgrade one part of your diet**. If you desire to eat healthier but don't know where to start, choose one thing. I know I love sugar, and don't feel good when I've eaten too much, so I chose to replace my afternoon sweet treat with fruit. I know, it's just what my mother would tell me to do. But guess what, she was right! And if I *don't* buy the sweet treats and *do*

buy some beautiful fresh oranges, then the choice is easy. I peel my chilled from-the-fridge orange and segment it onto a plate. I can then nibble away, receive yummy sweetness, and I have nourished my body too. It sounds so simple, and it is!

55. **Keep your mindset elevated**. Do whatever it takes to keep up your *that girl* demeanour. Read motivational quotes or whatever works for you. I have a document on my computer that I save quotes to as I come across them. Five minutes reading that document does wonders for my spirit. I feel motivated and reinspired. Find authors who make you feel happy and hopeful. Give yourself pep talks. Write the kind of inspiration you need to hear. Quality nutrition helps too. When I've had a junky food day, I feel low. But when I give myself good food, I feel amazing. Gather together everything that makes you feel fabulous and encouraged and remember to call on them.

56. **Create your *that girl* wardrobe**. What would you wear if you were your own dream girl? What would *she* wear? I often find it easier to approach questions from the 'she' angle. Then I can dream and imagine and plan my look. Of course, I'll shop my own closet first. Often it's just the action of wearing my

nicer things, and putting outfits together in different ways. And actually wearing the accessories I own rather than just looking at them hanging there. My beautiful scarves, changing out my handbag, and wearing different earrings than my usual pearl or 'diamond' studs. Getting into the 'How would *she* show up?' state of mind also makes me want to do more with my makeup, and style my hair differently than a ponytail which I wear most of the time at home. *She* is a great inspirer and motivator!

57. **Journal on your *that girl* lifestyle**. Create your own inspiration by noting in your journal all the ways 'she' would be. Here are a few notes from one of my sessions to inspire you: *She makes herself no. 1. She stays in her lane and focuses on what she wants to do. She prioritizes looking good, being healthy, dressing well, and her beauty and grooming. She chooses to glow from the inside out with juicy nutrition and clean living. She gets to have fun living her life. She decides that 'fun' for her is looking like a bombshell, having high standards, and kicking butt in her career. She loves being 'on point', whether it's her nails, how she dresses, her admin, laundry, or a tidy space. She keeps a minimal home and declutters regularly. She only looks forward, never back. She runs her own race.*

She loves abstaining, moderation, and the elegance of refusal. She quantum leaps when it comes to her goals, desires, and standards. When she puts her mind to something, she does it. She is kind on the outside, and unapologetic with her boundaries on the inside. She asks questions more than she talks. She loves fashion and pushes the edge when it comes to her personal style. She stands tall with confidence, and the posture of a ballerina. She has magnetism, allure, and mystique. How fun is that? And motivational too! Borrow mine or write your own.

58. **Keep life simple**. I do not believe you can adopt *that girl* energy with a complicated, exhausting daily existence. At least I don't believe I can, and I don't want to. My ongoing focus is to simplify my life – in the possessions I own, how I interact with people, the thoughts in my head, basically in every category I can think of. Not every season of life will be smooth sailing. We will all hit road bumps both big and small, with our health, in money situations or relationships, and even natural disasters like we experienced recently here where I live in Hawke's Bay, New Zealand. People lost their homes and in some tragic cases their lives from the devastating Cyclone Gabrielle. We had property damage but were lucky that our home was unaffected, however our power was

out for three weeks, and we had no running water for a month. And our internet took seven weeks to restore. Going through this reignited my desire to live a simple life, where there is less to take care of, less to lose. And when something huge such as a health scare comes along, living simply can lessen the burden when you need to redirect your energy into getting better.

59. **Dress up every day for no reason**. Because, why not? Why not make your everyday life your runway. Why not dress for your dreams. Why not be that person who people remember because she is always well turned out. It's not that you have to buy extra-fancy clothes, you can just wear what you've got, but use your nicer things. We all have clothes that we save for best, or slightly fancier occasions. And in my experience, I don't get my money's worth from these items because we don't have that many extra-special events to go to. The other day I met my husband Paul for lunch at a café near his work. I chose to wear a black cotton blouse with broderie puff sleeves with my white jeans and some summery yellow casual wedge sandals. I felt amazing! The only time I'd worn this blouse was to my sister's fiftieth birthday dinner two months previous. It was dressier than I'd normally wear during the day, but I didn't feel

out of place among the well-dressed office workers and stylish people out for lunch. It cost me nothing to dress like this, and I did feel very *that girl*. And all for a different blouse!

60. **Romanticize your life**. For those of us who are dreamers, and see everything through rose-tinted lenses, there is no better fun than seeing how romantic and fanciful we can make our chores and tasks. A woman I used to work with was a master at this without even knowing it. Everywhere she went, either at home or work was elevated by her magical touch. She just had a way of making everything sparkle. We can do this for ourselves too by looking to see how we can make anything pedestrian just a little more special. Can you try a different shower gel? Or laundry detergent? There are some really pretty scented ones around these days. Or can you make your bed with extra care and change out the decorative pillows you display? These seem basic, but I've found that it is the simple little things that make everyday living more enjoyable.

61. **Meal prep like *that girl* does**. I adore those images on Pinterest that show portion containers, one for each day of the week. One section might contain salad or crudités, another a serving of protein, and so on. They

look so neat and appealing with their bright colours. And imagine simply opening the fridge and taking one out for lunch each day. It would be easy to be healthy because the decision is already made. And that's the point! Even if you don't want to go out and buy meal prep containers, you can still prepare food ahead of time. Create appealing mini-meals for yourself and *make being healthy the easiest option*.

62. **Generate your own energy**. Make decisions throughout your day based on whether they will enhance or deplete your energy. Leaving a small job undone (energy draining) versus doing it straight away (energy increasing). Dwelling on negative thoughts versus giving yourself a pep talk. Doing a five-minute tidy or not. Having a short stretching session or sitting for hours at your desk. Even down to what snack you choose – a fresh piece of fruit or something processed from a foil wrapper. Spend just one day evaluating each choice and see how many micro-instances there are in which you can make a (compounding) difference. I promise you, from my experience there are a lot!

63. **Find your style of journalling**. There are many ways to journal, and if we want to be *that girl* in our own life, we know it's important to

our success to find one that resonates with us. You can try bullet journalling, scrapbook journalling, or follow a certain method such as *The Artist's Way* morning pages. Or, do as I do and DIY it. I love to make my own rules and do what I want. So, my journaling will be quite organic and vary from time to time. I'll write 'happy lists' of things that make me feel good (as detailed in Chapter 3 of my book *The Peaceful Life*), ask my future self for advice, write out my top ten desires or goals, and brainstorm inspiring lists from various journal prompts such as 'How can I make my everyday life easier?' or 'How would my idealistic Paris girl dress?' Just go with whatever you're in the mood for at the time and you can't go wrong!

64. **Identify your desired 'essence'**. How would you ideally like to be known? Can you come up with three descriptive words to describe how others could receive you? You don't need to limit yourself to three, you could dream up a beautifully long list to 'shop' from, but having three to focus on at any one time is easier. I would love people to see me as cheerful, positive, and capable. Or for my husband to see me as feminine, playful, and easy-going. There is something about coming up with your own essence words that helps keep your focus on what you want, not what you don't want. Sometimes I'll ponder, 'I don't

want them to think I'm overly picky or demanding', so instead will remind myself that I get to be perceived any way I like and choose something different such as calm, strong, and reasonable. What three words immediately come to mind for you?

65. **Dress well for exercise**. Typical *that girl* attire is athleisure – a pair of leggings and a pretty, sporty top. Perhaps, like me, your personal style does not have athletic wear as daytime clothing. But to encourage body movement, why not purchase some lovely pieces that you will be happy about wearing? Maybe it will lead to more activity such as a yoga class on YouTube or a walk in the sun with a podcast streaming. Every so often I'll buy some new workout clothes – mine aren't expensive, the leggings, tops and socks I wear are from Kmart and I have a few pairs of leggings from Victoria's Secret. But I like the colours, and they are comfortable. Plus, because they didn't cost a lot, I have multiples to always have a clean set on hand – five tops, a similar number of leggings, and eight pairs of socks. But what I did spend on was a pair of high-quality Asics walking shoes which make my feet happy. See if there are any barriers to you enjoying exercise more, and work on eliminating them. Perhaps proper work-out clothing is that barrier?

66. **Count your blessings**. In our modern world where many seem to feel entitled to everything, it is rare to come across someone who is thankful and humble. The key is to be that way while also having a sense of yourself, of knowing what you deserve. When you are thankful for everything in your life you will be richly rewarded, and more will come to you. Your energy will be magnetic to others, and you will be happier in yourself. Whenever you feel you might be becoming too expectant, switch back to gratitude. Be thankful. It will settle your soul in an instant.

67. **Make the most of your home life**. There is something about setting up our home to support us that really assists in us showing up as our best self. I always find it best when I 'stay at home more'. My thoughts are that when I am out, a lot of things fall behind at home. Of course, many of us must go to work, but if we have the choice in our leisure time, staying in feels wonderful. You get to be in your bliss at home, making your home life lovely, resting, feeling peaceful and keeping things nice. Meals are prepped earlier, and it really feels like you are living your dream life in your tidy and clean home. You get to use what you have, and then when you do go out, it's a bit of a treat. You really appreciate outings more!

68. **Be creative**. Take a little time every day to do something that activates the creative side of you. Find a pretty colouring-in book. Bake something. Sew, knit, crochet or work on a needlepoint piece. Tend to your herb, vegetable, or flower garden if you love the outdoors. Arrange flowers. Practice a musical instrument. Join a theatre company. Go to a ballet class. My sister paints art and has recently branched out into small jigsaw woodwork pieces that she paints – such as an animal or person likeness. Whatever appeals to you, find some small way you can incorporate it into daily life. Even if it's just appreciating that you enjoy being creative and going and taking a look at your current project before you leave for work that day!

69. **Wear beautiful pyjamas**. Just as you cultivate a more elevated self-image with the clothes you wear, so too can you make your night-time a place of pleasure and luxury. What would your *that girl* persona wear to bed? Mine would climb into a clean, white-sheeted cloud of a bed wearing a soft-toned (Blush pink? Sea glass blue?) silky chemise in the summer, and cozy man-style pyjamas in a silky fabric in the winter. Next time you need nightwear (or maybe you could use something new right now when you think of your current options...) let *that girl* lead the way. Let her

show you something new, something fresh, something fabulous.

70. **Approach everything in a low-key way**. Choose to be more productive at work, keep a tidier home, or be healthier *in a gentle, moderate way*. And why not? Why not do this in preference to pushing and hustling? Humans have a capacity for growth, by nature we always want to be improving and growing. But we can do this in a way that honours our delicate nervous system. We don't need to stress ourselves out in order to do better for ourselves. We can be the kind of person who puts relaxation and mental wellbeing first. That sounds far more enjoyable than a strict diet, a workout plan and whipping ourselves into shape. Next time you feel the urge to embark on a self-improvement project or have an area in your life that you wish to renew, approach it in a loosened, low-key way and see how much more enjoyable it becomes.

71. **Have glowing, moisturized skin**. *That girl* is all about self-care, and nothing says you look after yourself like having beautiful skin. Prioritize time to cleanse, tone and moisturize twice a day. I spend at least twenty minutes in the evening washing my face and I love it. It is my soothing wind-down time before bed. Nothing I use is expensive either. You don't

need to spend a lot of money in my opinion. I had a facial last week with a gift voucher and the beauty therapist raved about my skin. *It's so supple and soft!* she said. And it's all from 'little and often', plus, maybe a little genetic help. But you can't rely on genes, so pamper your skin twice a day and be rewarded with soft, glowy skin. Don't just do your face either. After your bath or shower moisturize your neck and décolletage, arms and shoulders, feet, legs and bum cheeks, and your stomach too. I do this every morning and it's such a lovely 'spa time' to start the day.

72. **Create your own plan**. The concept of being your own coach is such a fun one to consider. You get to look at yourself from the outside and make suggestions. You get to devise a bespoke plan of action to improve an area of your life. And you get to do all of this for free, in your own time. Journal prompts are a great way to do this, both answering questions plus dreaming up your own questions. Making a list of tasks for your homework is great too. If you've always wanted to write a book perhaps your first assignment could be coming up with ten or twenty possible book titles or ideas. Introduce yourself to... *yourself*, and see how you can set the world on fire with your brilliance.

73. **Read books that inspire you**. *That girl* is a reader, and she loves self-improvement and self-development books as well as fiction. Find authors who encourage you, rather than reading bossy, clinical books that make you feel 'less than'. If you have to push yourself to finish a book it's probably not the author for you. Reading books and re-reading old favourites is one of the many ways I feel inspired to write *my* books. They might not be directly related to my material and what I write about, but they make me feel good, positive, and happy. All of Rhonda Byrne's books do that for me, especially the audiobooks. They are a wonder!

74. **Brainstorm your ideal schedule**. How would you spend your day if you had the choice? I got to find this out after I become a self-employed work-from-home writer in 2016. My ideal day is very loosely structured. I don't do well with time blocking, strict schedules, and stop/start times. But I found I gravitated to writing early in the morning, as soon as I get up around 6am, for a few hours. Then I exercise and walk the dogs, have breakfast, shower, and get dressed for the day. I do household chores such as making my bed, laundry, and dinner prep. And I am always sneaking in some more writing. This works better for me than seeing in my planner:

'Writing: 8am-11am'. It's taken me trial and error to work these things out. Even if you work in a job, still ponder your preferred schedule, and work it in around what you have to do. And delight in it on weekends!

75. **Apply a facial mask once a week**. *That girl* is always shown with a sheet face mask, haven't you noticed? I have tried them, but I'm not a fan. I find them awkward to put on, unsettling to look at, and they are cold and clammy on your face. Plus, you throw the mask away afterwards so they're not exactly green. I prefer an old-fashioned paint-on mask where there is no waste. As with skincare, I don't believe you need to spend a lot of money. My current mud mask comes in a tube and is around $10 at the supermarket ('Mud Masque' from Skinfood, a New Zealand brand).

76. **Apply your mask with a brush**. Also, buy yourself an inexpensive paint brush to use; it makes all the difference. Mine is from a beauty supply store and the bristles are 1.5 inches long, and ¾ inch wide, just to give you an idea of size. I'm sure you could find one from a discount store, or even an art supply store. It doesn't need to cost a lot, just make sure it's not too soft and not too stiff. Right in between is perfect. I find that there is less wasted product when I paint my mask on, and it goes

on evenly too. I squirt the mud into my hand and paint it on from there. I'm telling you, you will feel like a professional painting your mask on, and it's easy to clean up too. My brush has been with me for close to twenty years, so the cost per use is minimal!

77. **Take a day off**. Everyone needs a vacation to avoid burnout. Even if it's only one or two days. Even if it's a staycation at home. Perhaps you feel like your weekends are just not cutting it at the moment, that they're just not enough. Put your mental health first and book one or two days off work. Maybe it won't be tomorrow, but can you apply for a day's annual leave soon? Know what you need to liven you up if you're feeling blah. Maybe it's just some space to read, relax, and *be*. Or maybe you know you'll feel better if you have some extra time to get your life in order. Or, if you're lucky enough to have room in your budget, how about a night away somewhere nearby? Where I live, we have multiple options within a few hours' drive. Imagine taking Friday off work and setting out on Friday morning. You'd stop for lunch somewhere, see the place where you've travelled to in the afternoon, stay in a nice hotel, and eat breakfast out the next day. You'd drive home on Saturday where you would still have almost a full weekend to

yourself. That is such a good payoff for one day's leave from work!

78. **Live a life of luxury**. A life of luxury isn't just about having endless funds to travel on super yachts and being able to hire an interior designer to do up your home. You can live a life of absolute bliss regardless of the amount of material things you own. In fact, for me, my ideal luxurious life has less. I imagine living in a spacious apartment with only my favourite things around me. And sure it's nice to have our comforts but when you think about it, the real luxury is in our mindset. We can sink back into our pillowy mind and luxuriate in our bliss by appreciating all that we already have. Make it known to yourself right now that you don't need material items to live a life of blissful luxury. You are claiming it right now, as you are. And so it is.

79. **Wear less makeup**. *That girl's* look is one of polished, glowy skin, the perfect cat-eye flick of liquid eyeliner, false lashes, groomed brows, and dewy lips. How I interpret this my way, appropriate to my own style and age group, is to wear less, and also to go for a cleaner look. It's fun to try different makeup looks, and I adore a light smoky eye in either navy or warm brown tones. However, when I'm being *that girl* for the day, I apply a small amount of

foundation with a damp makeup sponge. Bronzer and blush are used with a very light hand, and I wear minimal eye makeup, instead going for lashings of mascara. I also pencil my eyebrows lightly and brush them up. Take a look at a '*that girl* makeup' or '*clean girl* makeup look' tutorial on YouTube to get the general idea, and then adapt to suit you, your lifestyle, and your preferred look. Changing up your makeup is one of the many ways you can update your look, and appear more youthful too.

80. **Upgrade to healthy one step at a time**. *That girl* is all about being healthy, but I've found for myself that it doesn't work to make massive sweeping changes to my diet all at once. What ends up happening is that I snap back like a rubber band to how I used to eat... What works better for me is to make small changes and let them settle. This doesn't make my toddler mind rebel so much it seems. One example is that a bigger component of my meal is fresh now. I have smoothies for breakfast more than bagel and cream cheese. And I have far fewer sweet treats and potato chips than I used to. Find your areas – be a nutrition detective and view your diet as an outsider – and make plans to upgrade them in small ways.

81. **Indulge in solitude**. Perhaps it is driving to a nearby public park and strolling through the gardens with a coffee in hand. Or sitting outside a café with your journal and big sunglasses. Or going to a movie by yourself in the middle of the day. Hmm what do all these things have in common? You're by yourself. And that's what makes many of us feel self-conscious, like we have to have someone alongside us to do any of these things. Just for fun, this week, choose something to do by yourself. Find something you will really enjoy and do it. Thinking about my week coming up, the first thought that came to mind was going for a long walk along the waterfront and through town. About an hour or so. A *hot girl walk* of course! I'll dress for stylish exercise, put my headphones on and listen to something inspiring. Such fun!

82. **Try a three-month container**. Three months is the time of a season – right now we're entering autumn in New Zealand – and coincidentally three months is a popular goal-setting time-frame as well ('The 90 Day insert-goal-here Challenge'). Whatever season you are in while you are reading this book, choose a three-month time-frame to cultivate your *that girl* persona. Mine is going to be fall-flavoured and I'll be doing all the lovely, cozy things such as reading paper books under a

throw rug, going for long walks outside among the leaves, making slow cooker recipes and 'autumn-cleaning' my home. Approaching life like this brings a gentle, supportive pace and helps you achieve your goals without stress. And doesn't it just sound like a delicious way to live in general?

83. **Create your seasonal capsule**. As well as being seasonal in the way you live, make an effort to design your ideal wardrobe for the coming season. There is no need to go out and buy anything new, not yet at least. Go through your clothes to see if you can assemble an appealing collection, and hang them all together once you're done. See how the colours flow and contrast. Are you happy with what you see? Do they all fit you well? Are they in good repair? I know many of you do this already, but some of us need the reminder. Some of us go from one season to the next without taking inventory and then come unstuck at some stage! Changing for the new season is also a good opportunity to tidy your closet and refamiliarize yourself with what you already own before you go out shopping to fill in the gaps.

84. **Make decisions that leave you stress-free**. We all have decisions to make every single day. Sometimes they are in response to

others requests, and sometimes they originate as an idea we've had. Something that has been very helpful to me is to run them through my stress-filter. Basically, will this choice leave me more stressed and anxious, or less? It works well with the big decisions, and also right down to small ones, such as 'Shall I make my bed right now or leave it until later?' or 'Shall I catch up on my laundry or watch a movie?' *That girl* does everything she can to lower friction in her life because it just feels better. Follow her lead.

85. **Curate your *that girl* fridge**. If we peeked inside your fridge or freezer right now, what would we find? Would you be rushing to cover the doors so we couldn't see what's inside? I know there would be times when I would! I might have ice cream in the freezer (which means I will be eating it within the next twenty-four hours, ice-cream and I cannot have a simple relationship), and bags of frozen convenience foods too. And the pantry, don't get me started. Are there bags of potato chips hiding underneath? Sweets and chocolate up top? Something that inspires me to not restock the unhealthy stuff, is to imagine my *that girl* fridge. It would have eggs, milk and yogurt, and a multitude of fresh produce too. I would wash and prepare the vegetables so they are ready to make a salad or use in a stir-fry. My

fruit would be stacked enticingly and ready to eat. Find inspiring photos of healthy fridges on Pinterest and make yours the same. I don't mean with the matching container sets, but with the brightness of foodstuffs such as green and red bell peppers. Clean, and clean *out* your fridge regularly. Make it a goal to eat all your fresh food before the next grocery day. Filling yourself up with nutritious goodness all starts with an inspiring fridge!

86. **Recharge your battery**. Just like you'd plug your phone in at night, so too must you plug yourself in, lest you run out of battery. You might wonder why you're grabbing unhealthy snack foods and sweet treats but it's because you've got no charge left and you haven't got a power bank either! (Have you seen those? They are an extra battery you can leave charged in your bag to plug your phone into when it is running low.) Create a better 'power bank' for yourself by having a Ziploc bag of raw almonds in your purse, or preferably don't let yourself get to that low level in the first place. Put sleep, relaxation, and food first. If you're going out for the day, work out where you will eat, don't leave it to chance. Go to bed at a reasonable hour even if it feels 'boring'. And don't pack out your schedule so that there is no room to play. (A funny aside, my sister is gluten-free and vegan, and is very self-

sufficient since she never knows if there will be food to suit her. Recently she went to a wedding and told me that she packed a peanut butter sandwich in her evening bag just in case. How cute is that! And practical too!)

87. **Own your style**. Maybe you are drawn to the Cottagecore trend and have started adding Laura Ashley touches into your décor and personal style. Or you love playing around with your scrapbooks and creating inspiring pages. Whatever you love, enjoy it wholeheartedly. I am quite the geeky sort who was bookish as a girl and loved hobbies such as stamp collecting and weaving. I had my own small weaving loom from which I produced mismatched table mats (it was boring to make the same one twice), and even joined a stamp collectors club. I would go to meetings – me at around fourteen years old along with proper grown-up stamp people. My mother used to drop me off and pick me up since I wasn't old enough to drive. I mean really, joining the local philatelic society as a fourteen-year-old, it's not exactly what the cool kids do, right? But obviously that's what I was drawn to so why try and hide it? Now, I am proud of being me, of being different to others, and of having a unique perspective too. I have learned not to care what others think of my interests as well. So please, love what you love, because it's

awesome to be that way. Be you, every part of you. What you are drawn to *makes you you*. And you are the best!

88. **Look at what you outsource**. One of my personal definitions of *that girl* is that she is great with money. For myself, I love to do things to save money if it will be just as easy and the results are just as good. I tint my eyebrows at home every month, do my own manicures, make 99% of my own meals and prefer a delicious frothy coffee at home. For many years we had a weekly house cleaner, but now I prefer to do it myself. It just feels so good to be thrifty, and I love working towards our financial goals. And, when I do outsource things, I *really* enjoy them. I go for a massage or facial very occasionally, get professional pedicures in the summer, and I have highlights put into my hair four times a year. I also send my husband's business shirts out to be laundered. Your 'ins and outs' will be different, but look at your 'outs' and see if it would be just as nice to 'in' them. When you do this, saving money doesn't feel like a sacrifice, it feels like an *upgrade*.

89. **Age gracefully**. Yes, *that girl* is considered to be a young demographic, I get that. But I also believe we can be youthful as a state of mind as we get older. I am currently fifty-two and plan

on being *that girl* until I am very, very old! This translates into a flexible way of thinking and not being too rigid about my opinions and beliefs. It means choosing clothes, shoes, makeup, and accessories that while are still comfortable and a pleasure to wear, do not age me. And it also means I will consistently work towards being the healthiest version of myself, because life is just better when you're healthy, especially as you get older. There are many examples of stylish, chic, trim, and vibrant older ladies whether in the media or real life. Look to them for inspiration of how you could evolve into the next version of yourself.

90. **Form yourself**. Italian sculptor Michelangelo, creator of the statue David among other priceless pieces of art, was asked how he did it, how he had released this realistic-looking larger-than-life man from a block of marble. He said, 'I created a vision of David in my mind and simply carved away everything that was not David'. I keep this in mind when I clean, tidy and organize my home, when I am going through my closet, or when I am making a meal in the kitchen. Sometimes I think to myself, 'This is not the next level of *Fiona*. I am removing anything that is not the *Fiona* of the future from my life.' Those items go into a donation box, or I decide not to buy certain food items again. As you

create a fresh image of yourself, remove everything that is not *the new you* from your life. Reinvent yourself as you align with this vision. Let this thought effortlessly create bigger and better things!

91. **Plan little treats**. Just for fun, write down every single thing that makes you happy (and keep adding to your list as you think of others). If you can think of a million small things so much the better. Then, 'shop' from your list often. Rereading favourite books, having a petite stash of individually wrapped high-quality chocolates, wearing your more special blouses, deep conditioning your hair and blow-drying it silky smooth, having a manicure at home or out, buying a new magazine, going to a movie at the theatre – these are some of mine. All of our lists will look different, but the important thing is to come up with *your* bespoke treats menu and choose from it, daily.

92. **Edit your makeup collection**. Is it time to freshen up how you do your makeup? Take the opportunity to scrutinise your makeup collection. Are there old items to throw out? Can you clean up all the items you love and use and make them look brand new? Wash your makeup brushes and stand them in a clean glass. Then, look on YouTube for tips to

freshen up your look or even book in for a makeup counter makeover. As well, look at others to see if there are any looks you'd like to learn. Refreshing the way you do your makeup from time to time – it doesn't need to be anything too drastic – keeps you looking modern and it's also enjoyable. Your energy is elevated and putting your makeup on each morning seems more fun.

93. **Book in your birthday**. Prioritize yourself by making a big deal out of your birthday, even if that 'big deal' is simply a day to do as you please. I know some businesses who give each employee a day off on their birthday each year. Isn't that fabulous? What a morale-boosting initiative! I also know people who book a day's annual leave each year on their birthday. Do the same for yourself and make your day a special day of fun. You could spend it with others or designate it as a day of reflection where you look over the past year and design the next. (Did you know your birthday is your own personal new year?) Happy birthday to you!

94. **Make your bedroom your sanctuary**. How would that girl treat her bedroom? I can already see the aesthetic, of lots of white, blush pink and rose gold. There are framed inspirational slogans and a faux sheepskin on

her beauty seat. That's not the décor of my bedroom, and it might not be yours either, but we can still be inspired to create our own beautiful, peaceful haven to support us at the beginning, and the end of each day. We can simplify it, clean it, and set out little comforts such as a fluffy rug to wrap around our legs while we read, and I also like hand-made fabric coasters to put my water glass or teacup on. Change up your bedding if you have more than one set, move your pictures around so they appear new to your eyes, and remove anything that doesn't need to be in there. When I give my bedroom a freshen up I always feel more easily able to rest, and I feel energized too.

95. **Set up simple routines to support your life**. I have worked out a routine that I can keep my home looking presentable, comfortable and hygienic without exhausting myself with all-day cleaning marathons. It's the little-bit-each day approach which I know is common, however what made it personalised for me is that I took the five most important things and do one a day Monday to Friday. So simple! And would you believe it, I actually look forward to doing that day's task each day? Another routine is that I grocery shop on a Monday and only buy enough for that week because I prefer to keep a smaller amount of food on hand. Finding routines that

keep things ticking over while also enjoying yourself and having time for leisure, is key to living the good life for *that girl.*

96. **Do a life audit**. Just as an external consultant will go into a business to see if it is running at optimum levels, so too can you do an audit on your life. The goal is to become crystal clear on your priorities and values and ensure they align with how your daily life unfolds. Revisit *everything*. Look at who you follow online, what books you read and what movies or series you watch. Do they still resonate with you? Do your bookshelves still inspire you? Has your Instagram feed become too big and unwieldy? Consider a clean sweep unfollowing everyone and then building it up again, or starting a new account where you don't post, but simply follow who is currently inspiring you and keeping that list small. Go through every category in your life – your home, how you earn money, how you take care of your health, how you dress, your friends, and how you spend your free time. Imagine that you are moving to a new country and are starting over. You have a clean slate and could choose everything afresh. How would you live your life then?

97. **Build your own support team**. Think about celebrities, sports stars, or successful

businesspeople. They have a lot of support around them. Maybe they employ a personal masseuse, pilot, driver, hairdresser, chef, business manager, assistant or kinesiologist. What about you though, do you have a support team? And could you increase it? Right now I have an accountant, hairdresser, and supportive friends as well as my own 'success mindset'. Consider what your team looks like and see if there are any other areas in which you can be better supported. It doesn't have to cost much money at all, but it's a fun thing to consider – it just sounds so fancy to have a support team! And as well, you can feel more supported knowing these people are behind you, whether you know them or not. I count following a coach's YouTube channel and being inspired by their viewpoint as part of my support team, for example.

98. **Start your week with positivity**. Instead of grumbling like everyone else and heading into Monday with a sense of doom, switch it around. Look upon each week as a new beginning. Think what you want to achieve in that week, whether it's doing five minutes of yoga every day for seven days, or simply claiming calmness as a state of mind. It's fun to have active goals, but imagine having your goal for the week be: *I want to read every day, go to bed at a good hour, and feel peaceful*

most of the time. How glorious. However you dream your ideal week could look like, go into that week with a sense of promise, and sparkle. Enjoy being different to everyone else when they are stumbling to the coffee machine at work complaining how their weekend was too short. You know better, you get to have a beautiful week starting with Monday, and every day.

99. **Make the journey enjoyable**. Becoming your own version of *that girl* is actually a lot of fun when you are present and mindful about it. It's probably the best gift you could ever give yourself as a woman. Set it in your mind that you are going to have a blast today and every day as you develop yourself into the person you have always wanted to be. When you expect your growth and evolvement to be fun, it will be. It will never be hard or boring when you approach it from the right state of mind. Switch your focus to pleasure and curiosity, and you will wake up every day bouncing with energy. And even on the days when you aren't, you will still have hope and excitement.

100. **Start where you are**. This little book is chock full of ideas and tips, but I hope it doesn't overwhelm you or give you the sense of 'Fiona's so perfect, *la di dah*'. I have built up all these habits and ways of being over years,

not days, and I still have my off-moments where I flop around like a waste of space the whole day. All of us are only human, *and* we like to be inspired, I know I do. I love to dream of better days, even when today is perfectly fine and good. It's only natural to always want to be growing and thriving, and the best way to do this is from where you are today. Choose one or two inspired actions and go from there. Relax and find peace. Enjoy yourself as you make improvements to your lifestyle, your wardrobe, or your mealtimes. There is no hurry, no finish line and no pressure. Isn't that wonderfully soothing to hear?

At its core, the *that girl* lifestyle is about living our best life. It's about being healthy and productive. It's about being happy and successful. And it's about balance too. A balance of doing well and also of ultimate relaxation.

It's a blend of the masculine (doing) and the feminine (being). We need our masculine side to get things done, and we need our feminine side to enjoy ourselves and be able to rest.

We become best friends with our inner self when we connect regularly in journal time and maybe even meditation sessions. I haven't established a meditation routine but I do enjoy quiet time and love spending time in my journal.

We value success and happiness for ourselves and others. Nothing makes us more delighted than when we see others creating good things in their life too.

We do what makes us happy *and* we're kind people.

We help others without burning ourselves out.

There is so much goodness to come when we designate ourselves to be our own... *that girl.*

50 Ways to be
your own Main Character

And to finish, as well as thank you for reading this book, please enjoy this bonus chapter – fifty ways to be the main character in your own life – just as *that girl* is.

Being the main character is a fun concept I came across and it really tickled my fancy. I love romantic comedy movies with their idealistic portrayals of life, perfect city apartments and uplifting soundtracks. Spending an hour or two watching these movies always made the world seem a better place and like I could achieve anything.

I always have music playing at home, and sometimes when I heard a particularly good piece it felt like that music was a movie soundtrack, and that I was living in a movie. *Et voilà*, along came the main character trend. I'm telling you; I was all over it. It was my jam!

To me, being the main character in your life is all about:

- *choosing what you want* rather than always deferring to others.
- *owning all of you*, especially the parts that you think others will judge you for.
- living your life *by your own design*.
- *having the courage* to make big, life-changing decisions.
- having the guts to *go for what you want*.
- flavouring the way you live life in *your own preferred taste*.

And out of this comes *confidence*. The confidence to *enjoy being you*, and to own every part of yourself, the good *and* the 'bad'.

Fun articles online talk about harnessing 'main character energy' when you need to show up as your most confident self, such as going on a job interview, a date, or making a presentation at work. There are endless scenarios where it would be helpful to take on this persona.

I always love to finish my books with an inspiring list, so to finish this book I present to you *fifty ways to be your own main character*. I hope you enjoy the concept as much as I do, and that you find one or two tips to embody straight away. And, that you have fun with it as well!

1. **Focus on your good points** rather than dwell on all you could do better at. I know this is so basic, but some of us (me!) need constant reminders. It's simple, but it makes a huge difference to both your mindset and your actions.

2. **Say no when you want to say no**. You can communicate it in a soft way but still stand up for yourself. If you need a buffer before you say no, ask if you can think about it or say you need to check your schedule.

3. **Stay in your own story**. If you want everyone to like you this means you are wanting to be the main character in other people's stories. Stay in *your* story, *your* life, it's too exhausting otherwise. The only person's opinion you can control is your own – focus on that.

4. **Focus on the bright spots in your day**. Just like the lead actress in a romantic comedy movie who smells her coffee before she drinks it and stops to pat a cute dog at the park, so too can you enjoy those little micro-moments of joy. Let nothing be too small to take pleasure from.

5. **Start your day with your dreams**. You might not have time for a full-on journalling session, but at least take a moment to keep your goals in focus as you begin your day. Flip through your journal or have a written list or statement on a pretty card by your bed.

6. **Accept that you're not perfect** and be okay with that. Everyone makes mistakes, sometimes huge ones. The most important thing is that you learn from them, give yourself grace, and move forward.

7. **Consider your life as a glittering movie-montage**. What kinds of activities would it show you doing? How would you look? Who are you with? It's a fun visualization exercise to do for a few minutes and to imagine what your movie would look like. And, would it be a comedy? A romantic comedy? An intellectual feast? So many options!

8. **Stop criticizing**. When you criticize others, you are really criticizing yourself. What you notice in others (good or bad), dwells in you too. Let judgement pass you by and instead *focus on the good* in others, and yourself. It will take practice but it's worth it.

9. **Change your story**. You don't have to live in the past and bring along every unfair thing that

has ever happened to you. You can leave all of that behind and reinvent yourself, stepping forward from today as day one. *Who do you want to be today and from now on?*

10. **Be respectful of other's 'movies'.** You are the main character in your own movie, but so is everyone else, in theirs. You are all bit parts in each other's movies as you interact throughout the day, whether you know them well or are just passing.

11. **Be a benevolent character in your movie.** Imagine being the kind of lady who is strong, firm, and kind. She is always ready to help out another, but not at the expense of her own peace of mind, finances, or energy. She is a good person *and* has boundaries. We all need both.

12. **Take a YOU day.** Spend one whole day if you can, focusing on your values and nurturing yourself. Some of my values are creativity, health, and inner peace, so these would shape what self-care I'd choose to partake in on my free day.

13. **Light up when you talk to people.** Really listen to them and take them in. Become known as a great conversationalist and caring person all from the simple act of taking an interest in others.

14. **Work with what you've got**. Being your own main character means taking the raw material (you) and making the most of what nature gave you. Learn how best to style your own type of hair, and study makeup tutorials to best enhance your features if you like to wear makeup. Be the best version of *you*, not a copy of someone else.

15. **Be a positive person**. When you're the main character you dress in a colourful coat and go for a walk in the snow. You twirl around in the park catching snowflakes on your tongue. You wrap your hands around a hot coffee and savour the warmth and flavour. You look for the best in any situation and extract every ounce of pleasure. Okay, maybe I'm playing it up a bit, but surely looking for the positive anywhere you go can't help but make you a happier person!

16. **Be optimistic**. In the same vein, expect things to always work out for you. And they will! You expect to get the carpark, the unadvertised discount, and for the Universe to have your back. Make it a fun game, just like Pollyanna, to find the best in every situation. In 'bad' situations, ask yourself, 'Why is this a good thing?' and look for ten ways that it is.

17. **Surround yourself with positive people**. Equally important as being positive yourself, is

to be around 'can do' people. Don't try to change negative people, just limit the amount of time you spend with them. Look for like-minded people so you can influence and help each other, even if it's only online.

18. **Cultivate resilience**. Be the kind of person who is always moving forward. Don't let mistakes or setbacks derail you. Choose to learn from any situation you are in and to *keep on going*.

19. **Reinvent yourself regularly**. Who wants to always be the same, doesn't that sound so staid? Consider yourself flexible in your mind and always be open to change. Aim to be made of feathers and a light breeze instead of rigid wood and concrete.

20. **Do your inner work**. Any self-development work is useful because it educates you about yourself and your motives. Ask yourself questions in your journal and answer them. Make up questions you'd like to know the solutions to, and then answer those too!

21. **Don't be a victim** and don't be available for others victimhood. Something I really can't stand is victim energy, so I banned it in myself. I take responsibility for my own circumstances, and if it's a terrible situation like our recent

devastating cyclone, I just get on with things. I look for the next task I can do rather than sitting around wallowing and saying, 'It's so unfair'.

22. **Think *fresh, new, and exciting*.** Imagine approaching life from this perspective. Wouldn't it zing things up for you? It does for me. I prepare different meals, dress better, eat healthier, and go for a longer walk than usual, and all with a happy spirit.

23. **Be your own cheerleader** and pep-talker. Sometimes when I know I'm not at my full potential; maybe I'm moping around the house with my gears stuck in neutral (or worse, reverse!), I say gently, 'Come on Fiona, let's get going! Let's make the bed then write a chapter.' And I'm off, moving around and making things happen. It works!

24. **Sentimentalize everything about your life**. Because, why not? Be the heroine in one of your favourite novels. Enjoy your morning coffee in a pretty cup. Take a warm, sweetly-scented shower and apply a face mask. Surround yourself with tones of your favourite colour whether it's in your home or your mind.

25. **Write your own happy ending**. You don't have to go along with everything that's already happening. You can choose your own story and

how it ends too (happily ever after, of course!). Keep that beautiful vision in mind and work towards it. If you are a catastrophist like I can be, it's a really helpful tip to trick your sometimes negative mind.

26. **Trust that you are exactly where you need to be right now**. You don't have to worry about having missed your chance in life or that one shot at happiness. I see how this might appear to be at odds with writing your own happy ending, but they both work beautifully together: Be present and full of faith, *and* direct your story along the path you desire. Be someone who is trusting now, *and* shaping your own future.

27. **Be someone new**. Why not switch things up? Transform yourself? Have a makeover? Make it fun using items you already own, and bring a renewed energy. Smile, look up, dream of a new way of being. What category immediately comes to mind for you?

28. **Have a strong mental game**. Yes it's nice to dress well and look good, but concerning yourself with how others view you should never play a role in your own personal self-esteem. Whatever you need to feel good at the time, tomorrow or today, that's what you need to be doing. And disregard others' opinions about any of it!

29. **Be unpredictable**. People will become bored with you if you are too predictable. If you are a little *unpredictable* it is exciting to them plus scares them a little too. They will wonder why you are different, and be intrigued as well.

30. **Live in the present**. As much as possible, be here, today. You may look back with fondness or dream of the future and aim for that, but don't lose sight of today. Today is the best thing that ever happened to you. Channel yourself as the main character in your movie and *live this moment out loud*.

31. **Stop caring what other people think** and live the life you want to live. It really can be that simple but we complicate things a lot sometimes. I know I do!

32. **Look your best**. Put on makeup every day, smell good, be well groomed, and have nice nails. Whatever makes you feel fabulous, do it. These are my things, what are yours?

33. **Play different characters for fun**. Imagine channeling someone else for the day, an event, or even a weekend away. A good actress will melt into her role. Choose your flavour of main character and *act as if*. Pack what she would wear, think how she would interact with others.

Be your ideal self with the added *frisson* of a little extra flavouring!

34. **Expect to be blessed** and you will be. Have an air of positivity and always anticipate fortune to be on your side. Look for all the ways in which you are naturally fortunate and have the mantra for yourself of 'I am so lucky! Let good luck and happiness become the norm for you.

35. **Mirror how someone acts**. Let's say one of your friends is a bit distant; my natural inclination would be to wonder what I've done wrong. A better way to behave is to mirror their energy. Be busy doing your own thing – happy but busy – and let them come looking for you if they want to. Maybe they will and maybe they won't, and that's okay. *You will be fine either way.*

36. **Take personal responsibility**. Empower yourself by taking full accountability for your actions. You are a product of the choices you made. Don't try to lay the blame for *anything* on anyone else. Enjoy the feeling that comes with being fully in charge of your own destiny. Try it on for size – it feels amazing, doesn't it! And, now you've done that, you get to steer your future.

37. **Be happy-go-lucky**. Don't be concerned about the things you used to be concerned about. Don't hold on so tightly. Let everything be free and easy. Let the energy flow and feel any pressure on you lift. You don't have to be responsible for everything in life.

38. **Practice gratitude every day**. Speak 'thank you, thank you, thank you' out loud when something good happens. Make a 'Thank you' list (I write 'Thank you for...' and keep on going until one journal page is filled). It sounds trite but I promise you will feel amazing when you've finished, and it only takes a few minutes. Do some form of gratitude every day and you will feel like you are the luckiest girl in the world with *the* most amazing life.

39. **Step into the spotlight**. Don't let fear stop you from becoming the main character in your movie. Ask yourself what's the worst that could happen if you showed up *fully you*. People might get to know you better? Understand you more? If there is a downside, it's not worth the cost of you not showing up in your own life.

40. **Stop people pleasing**. Did you know that when you are always bending to others, you are actually wanting control over them? When I thought about it, it was true for me. So I stopped trying to ~~help~~ control others and worried about

myself, because I'm not so perfect either. When I did this, life became *so* much more relaxing.

41. **Be the author of your life**. If you don't like the way the story is going, write the next chapter differently. You have the ability to shape it into whatever you want it to be. Even with other people in your story, you can still adjust how *your* character behaves.

42. **Choose a pet name** and calm or cheer yourself as needed. I quite like 'babe' or 'Fifi'. 'Come on babe, let's go for a walk in the sun and then we'll get back to the computer' or 'It's only an hour until dinner Fifi, don't get the snacks out, you'll ruin your meal'. Be the mother to yourself with your pet names. I can imagine the lead in a romantic comedy doing this!

43. **Be self-possessed**. Some say the main character energy trend is an excuse to be self-centred. But I say adjust that to being *self-possessed*, being someone who is in control of their life.

44. **Curate your movie soundtrack**. Set the mood with music, whether it's peaceful spa music in the evening as you get ready for bed, top 40 while you are driving in your car, or cool *Hôtel Costes* vibes at dinner. Nothing makes a 'scene' better than the perfect music.

45. **Choose confidence**. It really is as simple as a decision sometimes. And if 'confidence' doesn't ring your bell, try a different guiding word such as certainty, courage, fortitude, spunk, or aplomb! Imagine starting your day with aplomb; that would end up being an epic day, right?

46. **Talk less**. Ever notice in a movie that when the main character is babbling it's because she is nervous or she's made a boo boo? And when she is in her power she is serene, self-assured and *not* talking so much? Be that calm, in control lady by talking less and listening more. (I still need to practice this every. single. day.)

47. **Be your best every time you step out the front door**. Don't let life pass you by. Life is short, very short. Dress up, smile, greet the day. It's not about looking younger; it's about looking good.

48. **Be unbothered**. You have no idea how much better your life gets when you stop caring. When you stop caring about things that are not beneficial to you, everything improves. Your attention is no longer on anything negative, it's all on *you*, and so you blossom.

49. **Dress your character**. Choose an outfit *she* would wear, or even more fun, make a capsule

collection for the whole 'movie'. Perhaps your character lives in NYC and is a successful florist. How would you dress her if you ran the wardrobe department? Mine might be an author who lives in Paris! What's your character today?

50. **Live in a fantasy world every day**. *That* is how you can create the world you want to live in!

To Finish

Thank you for reading *100 Ways to be That Girl*. It has been *so much fun* to write this book for you. In fact, a blast. I got to be a little over-the-top and tongue-in-cheek, but also, it's real. Deep down surely we all would love to be *that girl* radiating main character energy! Life is too short not to have a little fun from time to time.

I sincerely hope you gained inspiration from these pages to cultivate exactly how *that girl* would show up and style *your* life, as well as encouragement to dream up your most wonderful daily experience and enjoy living it.

If you have a moment, I would be beyond grateful if you could leave me a review on Amazon. Even a few words are perfect – you don't have to write a lot. A review is the best compliment you can give to an author. It helps others like yourself find my books, and I'd love to get my message of living well through an inspired mindset to as many ladies as possible.

And if you have anything you'd like to say to me personally, please feel free to write:

fiona@howtobechic.com

Maybe you have a book idea for me, want to let me know what you thought of this book, or have even spotted an error. I hope not, but if you do find a typo, please let me know!

Think of me as your friend all the way over in New Zealand, cheering you on and wishing you well. You can add as many fun and fabulous details as you like into your daily life. No-one else gets to have an opinion on any of this except for you. Why not live a life filled with every delight you could ever dream of? That's what it feels like when you become *that girl.*

With all my best to you, and I look forward to seeing you in my next book!

Fiona

About the Author

Fiona Ferris is passionate about the topic of living well, in particular that a simple and beautiful life can be achieved without spending a lot of money.

Her books are published in five languages currently: English, Spanish, Russian, Lithuanian and Vietnamese. She also runs an online home study program for aspiring non-fiction authors.

Fiona lives in the beautiful and sunny wine region of Hawke's Bay, New Zealand, with her husband, Paul, their rescue cat Nina, rescue dogs Daphne and Chloe, and their cousin Micky dog.

To learn more about Fiona, you can connect with her at:
howtobechic.com
fionaferris.com
facebook.com/fionaferrisauthor
twitter.com/fiona_ferris
instagram.com/fionaferrisnz
youtube.com/fionaferris

Fiona's other books are listed on the next page, and you can also find them at:
amazon.com/author/fionaferris

Other books by Fiona Ferris

Thirty Chic Days: *Practical inspiration for a beautiful life*

Thirty More Chic Days: *Creating an inspired mindset for a magical life*

Thirty Chic Days Vol. 3: *Nurturing a happy relationship, staying youthful, being your best self, and having a ton of fun at the same time*

Thirty Slim Days: *Create your slender and healthy life in a fun and enjoyable way*

Financially Chic: *Live a luxurious life on a budget, learn to love managing money, and grow your wealth*

How to be Chic in the Winter: *Living slim, happy and stylish during the cold season*

How to be Chic in the Summer: *Living well, keeping your cool and dressing stylishly when it's warm outside*

A Chic and Simple Christmas: *Celebrate the holiday season with ease and grace*

The Original 30 Chic Days Blog Series: *Be inspired by the online series that started it all*

30 Chic Days at Home: *Self-care tips for when you have to stay at home, or any other time when life is challenging*

30 Chic Days at Home Vol. 2: *Creating a serene spa-like ambience in your home for soothing peace and relaxation*

The Chic Author: *Create your dream career and lifestyle, writing and self-publishing non-fiction books*

The Chic Closet*: Inspired ideas to develop your personal style, fall in love with your wardrobe, and bring back the joy in dressing yourself*

The Peaceful Life*: Slowing down, choosing happiness, nurturing your feminine self, and finding sanctuary in your home*

Loving Your Epic Small Life*: Thriving in your own style, being happy at home, and the art of exquisite self-care*

The Glam Life*: Uplevel everything in a fun way using glamour as your filter to the world*

100 Ways *to Live a Luxurious Life on a Budget*

100 Ways *to Declutter Your Home*

100 Ways *to Live a European Inspired Life*

100 Ways *to Enjoy Self-Care for Gentle Wellbeing and a Healthy Body Image*

100 Ways *to Be a Chic Success and Create Your Dream Life*

Printed in Great Britain
by Amazon

47510964R00057